1 8 JUN 2022 WITH

rural children,
rural church

York St John

3 8025 00508462 2

Other titles in this series

Children and Bereavement
2nd edition

Wendy Duffy

Not Just Sunday
Setting up and running mid-week clubs for children

Margaret Withers

Special Children, Special Needs
Integrating children with disabilities and special needs into your church

Simon Bass

Where Two or Three
Help and advice for churches with few or no children

Margaret Withers

mission opportunities
in the countryside

rural children, rural church

YORK ST. JOHN
COLLEGE LIBRARY

Rona Orme

CHURCH HOUSE
PUBLISHING

Church House Publishing

Church House

Great Smith Street

London SW1P 3NZ

ISBN 978-0-7151-4126-7

Published 2007 by Church House Publishing

Copyright © The Diocese of Exeter 2007

All rights reserved. No part of this publication may
be reproduced or stored or transmitted by any means
or in any form, electronic or mechanical, including
photocopying, recording, or any information storage
and retrieval system without written permission which
should be sought from the Copyright and Contracts
Administrator, Church House Publishing, Church
House, Great Smith Street, London SW1P 3NZ
Tel: 020 7898 1451; Fax: 020 7898 1449
email: copyright@c-of-e.org.uk

Cover design by S2 design and advertising

Printed by Creative Print and Design Group

Blaina, Wales

Contents

Acknowledgements

I would like to thank everyone who has generously given time, thought and ideas to this book. I have been greatly encouraged by all the exciting stories of children's work happening in rural areas across the country. Thank you!

I have learned so much through developing 'Service with a Smile' ☺ (see chapter 5) with the help, generosity and commitment of so many people. Thanks are particularly due to Revd Douglas Dettmer for his vision and support.

Most of all, I would like to thank Revd John Congdon. He discerned my vocation to work with children soon after I came to faith. His quiet encouragement has led me to have far more fun, try new ideas and enthuse more people than either of us could ever have imagined, so many years ago.

Foreword

This book is all about finding ways of building relationships with children and families. It's also based on real experience with real children in real rural churches.

Rona Orme knows the rural background and its specific difficulties, and summarizes the current rural situation as it might appear to a child. To many children the 'rural idyll' is anything but. The reality is often isolation and a lack of the opportunities enjoyed by children in urban and suburban areas. Children make up 20 per cent of the rural population and need to be fully part of the Church's life. The reduced number of paid clergy available to rural areas has led to a crisis of confidence in many parishes. Even with the growth of other self-supporting lay and ordained ministries, work with children sometimes falls down the list of priorities. Yet research has proved that working with children actually sustains and enhances church life, even in very small rural communities.

The ideas in this book are not just ideas. They are drawn from real examples here in Devon and in other parts of the country. They are not just fun and imaginative: Rona is very well aware of all the practical considerations, from CRB checks to refreshments and lavatories, to be taken into account when working with children. So, please try some of them! They are imaginative, they are fun and they work!

Michael Langrish

Bishop of Exeter

Introduction

Many rural churches are finding a new role and a new purpose at the beginning of the twenty-first century and rural congregations are well placed to react to the changes in village life. You may have picked up this book for a number of reasons. Maybe you already have a vision for reaching out to children and their families and are looking for ideas. Maybe you are concerned at the few children in your church and you want to see their number grow. This book will give you many ideas for 'being church', particularly with children, in a rural setting. It is full of tried-and-tested ideas from other rural churches that have seen the importance of working with children in their area.

Some suggestions are tiny acts of outreach, and some will require the whole congregation to change its outlook. Many ideas will involve the church going out into the community, and some will invite the community into the church.

Children were at the heart of Jesus' ministry, and we must ensure that we place them at the heart of our ministry. This book will help you to think afresh about how children's work is regarded and organized, if at all, in your church.

The shape of this book

After an introduction to the rural church today, the ideas are divided into three sections:

- **Times and seasons** sharing the Church's year with the community, and the community's year with the Church;
- **Rites of passage** reaching children and their families at significant moments in their lives;
- **Belonging and being** the Church as both gathering point and contributing partner in the community.

Chapter 5, 'Encouragement from a small Devon parish', is the recent story of my own home parish.

Using the question sections

Not all the ideas in the book will work in your situation, but I hope that you will be inspired to adapt them – and ultimately to come up with your own – to suit the particular needs of your locality. Questions are included at the end of each chapter to help you and your PCC, or group of children's workers, to think through how you can apply the ideas presented here to your own situation.

The genesis of this book

The impetus for this book was the involvement of the Diocese of Exeter in Project REACH (Resourcing Evangelism Among Children), an initiative of the Archbishop's Officer for Evangelism Among Children. The five dioceses that took part in the project were encouraged to identify effective ways of reaching out to children and to find ways of sharing this information. There were five focus areas nationally:

- developing work with under-fives and their parents;
- putting children's ministry into parish development programmes;
- encouraging evangelism through holiday and midweek clubs, and children's community activities;
- working creatively on the relationships between parishes and local schools;
- improving the evangelistic aspect of good quality all-age worship, and other services.

Nationally, it was discovered that nearly 50 per cent of all work with children happens midweek rather than on a Sunday – but it may not be 'counted' by parishes and diocesan authorities. Everywhere, clergy, lay readers and especially children's workers flocked to training events. The Project REACH banner gave new credibility to the importance of children's work. In the Diocese of Exeter, a number of parishes were encouraged to try new outreach activities and now report an increased confidence in trying something new.

Hallmarks of success

The ideas and resources in this book have come from churches and communities in rural areas where children's work is starting to grow. Some places are seeing their first green shoots, whilst others could be described as starting to flourish. Each community has faced different problems and come up with different solutions, but there are a number of hallmarks of their success:

- the church has accepted the need for change;
- the church has been willing to put the needs of the children and families they hope to reach before their own needs and preferences;
- church members have been willing to plant a new 'congregation' or to accept radical change to their services, and to expect less for themselves;
- the church has listened carefully to what the community wants and tried to meet its need, rather than imposing its own agenda;
- the church has built careful links, often over many years, with other community organizations and events to earn confidence;
- the church has encouraged the development of lay leadership;
- the parish priest has been willing to share, or even delegate, responsibility for outreach in a particular location;
- the church has put the focus on a particular age-range of children in the first instance;
- a few people, not necessarily considering themselves to be children's workers, have been prepared to 'give it a go'.

The real battle for children being part of the church, however, is not about finding workers to lead children's groups or establishing more accessible worship. It is about changing the hearts and minds of long-term Christians who wish to maintain the present traditions to a point that they lose sight of the Church's mission among the youngest and most vulnerable generation.

There is one further reason why churches in hamlets and small villages should make it a priority to work actively with children. Research has proved that working with children sustains and enhances church life, even in very small rural communities[1]. It shows fruit in the number of infant baptisms, teenage confirmations and adult church attendance.

St Peter said:

The promise [of the Holy Spirit] is for you and your children and for all who are far off – for all whom the Lord our God will call.

Acts 2.39

I hope you will feel inspired to try some of the ideas in this book. I am passionate about encouraging churches to reach out to the children in their communities, and I pray that these pages will help you to catch some of this enthusiasm.

1 Rural church today

What is it like to live in a village these days?

It has got lots of space. Rhys, 7

Television sitcoms and early-evening dramas continue to show a stereotype of village life in which

- everyone lives in a thatched cottage;
- villagers have little knowledge of the outside world;
- every villager is a larger-than-life character;
- everyone knows everyone else intimately;
- residents live in the same village, and probably the same cottage, for life;
- cows walk through the streets;
- there is always a shop and a pub for everyone to meet and gossip in;
- church is a source of peripheral fun.

Reality is a little different. The quality and type of housing varies widely. Villagers watch television, and surf the Internet, as avidly as their suburban cousins. In many villages, houses change hands as rapidly as in the suburbs. Some are snapped up as second homes, some by commuters and some by people wanting to downshift to the 'good life'. Few young people can afford to rent or buy property in their village of birth, and the population is ageing. Only 11 per cent of the rural population are aged between 18 and 29 years, compared with 16 per cent in urban areas.[1] In other areas, housing is run down and of poor quality. Many people feel isolated and may not know their neighbours. Many farms have withdrawn from dairy farming so that the rhythm of life has changed. Numerous rural post offices and shops have closed, and many pubs are scarcely viable. The church may be the only public meeting place left in some communities. Many people living in a village have a marked sense of ownership of the church even if they rarely visit it or attend services. Some will express strong views on the activities that take place in it, both worship and social, even if they choose not to attend,

because they regard it as 'their' church. Before we go on to examine this
reality in more detail, it may be helpful to provide some definitions.

What is 'rural'?

When the traffic comes, it goes too fast. Rhys, 7

There is no one way to describe rural life. For some people, living a rural life
means they choose to live in a remote hamlet or isolated cottage. Others
choose to live in a village of between one and two thousand residents so
that there will be a reasonable range of services and activities. Yet more live
in market towns with many of the familiar patterns of urban life including
cafés, sports facilities and a choice of shops. Some people choose to live
in a village so they can feel they belong to a real community. Others prefer
to hide away in the countryside to avoid other people to a large extent.

So what is meant by 'rural'? Nearly 20 per cent of the national population
is regarded as 'rural'. The government regards any settlement of fewer than
10,000 people as rural, but this may not match the perception of those
living in the countryside. Since 2004 the government has subdivided its
rural definition between 'sparse' and 'less sparse' in recognition that the
population density of an area has an impact on the quality of life for residents.[2]

For example, in the district council area of mid-Devon, only the town of
Tiverton with a population of over 18,000 meets government guidelines as
an urban community but not all the residents of the small one-time market
towns of Crediton or Cullompton would describe themselves as living in a
rural area. In church terms, congregations in these market towns have a very
different experience from churches in Devon 'villages'; they may have an
average congregation size of more than 100. The vast majority of rural
people in the UK live in settlements of fewer than 1,000 people.

Amongst children under the age of 18, 1.7 million live in the country.
Generally, children make up nearly 20 per cent of the rural population.[3]

What is it like to be a rural child?

I don't think there are any bad bits about living in a village.

Lloyd, 9

Children are rarely given any choice in where they reside. Although government statistics show many rural areas to be relatively wealthy, overall figures often hide the fact that many rural children live in families that experience social exclusion.[4] It should be noted that fewer rural children live in lone-parent households than their urban cousins, one possible cause of social exclusion, though many children divide their time between two households if their parents have separated. They lack easy access to transport, sports facilities, leisure activities and shops. Rural children may have more freedom to roam, but there are often few places to go. They cannot just decide to buy some sweets or rent a DVD as there may be no shop to visit and no bus to take them. Few activities take place close to home. Many children are transported some distance to school by car or bus so that friends may live several miles away. There may be few children of the same age or gender at a small primary school so they can exercise little choice over friends. A few children positively dislike the isolation of village life and long to move closer to shops, entertainment and 'life'.

In terms of communications, Internet connections are improving but some villages have poor mobile phone coverage. Some children have to go outside and walk up the hill to be able to access a mobile phone signal.

Those who live in urban areas may see a childhood in the countryside as idyllic and isolated from the stresses and strains of city living, but many children are disturbed by the experience of living through a foot-and-mouth epidemic, the effects of bovine tuberculosis or the threat of an outbreak of avian flu. Eighteen per cent of the rural population (2.6 million people) live in low-income households; 700,000 children (23 per cent of rural children) live in poverty, and this represents 18 per cent of all poor children in the UK. Government initiatives to improve provision for children such as Sure Start and Children's Centres usually develop from an urban model so that they are much more difficult to implement in the countryside.[5] For example, most urban or suburban Children's Centres are based in a school or health centre. Many of those being developed in rural areas have no physical base and must be regarded as 'virtual' centres with the various professionals visiting the area. They do not offer a gathering place for residents, with the mutual support that would bring.

Being Christian in a rural area

This is my church! Phoebe, 3

The proportion of people who regard themselves as Christian, at least as far as answering the census goes, is higher in rural areas. Nearly 79 per cent of rural residents described themselves as Christian in the 2001 census, nearly 10 per cent more than among urban residents.[6] At the same time the proportion of Buddhists is higher in the countryside. This suggests either that people living in the countryside have a greater interest in spirituality, or that followers of Buddhism choose to drop out of urban life to follow their religion in what they perceive to be more favourable surroundings.

In villages, churchgoers are usually well known as such. They cannot hide their faith, and other residents may form their opinion of church or Christianity on the basis of their attitudes and behaviour. This can be a pressure for Christian villagers and a source of tension. Non-churchgoers can be puzzled by the existence of different denominations in a village and their perceived disunity. Others regard churchgoers as members of a threatening, impenetrable clique within the community.

Challenges for the rural church

The number of paid clergy and ministers has declined sharply in rural areas in recent years, and continues to fall in many dioceses. This has caused a crisis of confidence for many parishes so that work with children has sometimes fallen down their list of priorities. Many of the tasks undertaken by the clergy have now become tasks undertaken by lay people. Those with spare time, who might previously have worked with children, may now be called upon to become the parish treasurer, buildings officer or rota organizer. Some churches have debated the issue and decided it is better to work with children, and give less attention to the building. Yet others have decided to aim to become 'centres of excellence' for children's work, whilst acknowledging that they put little energy towards social justice campaigns or working with other groups of the population. Small churches are increasingly prepared to accept that they cannot do everything and that it is better to do a few things well.

Who does children's work?

Rural ministry is still often seen as a role for older clergy, or for younger clergy with sufficient energy to care for several parishes. In many places the merger of parishes has caused a crisis of confidence or an overburdening of leaders. In the past children's work might have been regarded as the job of the clergy, particularly a curate, whether or not they had aptitude for the task. The amalgamation of parishes means that the laity has recognized that children's work needs to be organized differently. Some churches have decided to employ a paid children's worker, even for just a few hours per week. However, even if a church can raise the necessary funds for a paid worker, the support and active involvement of volunteers will still be needed. In many places, Sunday morning has become the meeting time for sports clubs so that churches have had to find new slots in the week to work with children and families. Some churches have started to provide a Family Service at 5 p.m. on a Sunday afternoon at a time when many families are arriving home after a weekend of activity,[7] though this does not meet the needs of dairy farming families. In other communities midweek occasions are a better option for most people.

Who then can do this vitally important work? Many people consider that children's leaders need special skills and gifts. Some congregations are, indeed, blessed with people who are exceptionally talented at working with youngsters. Such people prefer chatting to children than to adults, they enjoy children's activities and they get excited about the possibilities. They love organizing parties, outings and exciting things to do. They are comparatively few in number and they are worth 'far more than rubies' – they deserve all the support and encouragement possible. In order for them to exercise this valuable ministry, they should be excused from taking on any other responsibility in the church.

Other congregations look to teachers and pre-school workers to work with children. They bring the benefits from all the professional and vocational training they have received, even if for some of them, their theological and faith development may not yet be mature. If they can be persuaded to help, they will organize activities that take into account the different stages and elements of child development, but it may be fair to allow them to have a break from their day job in their church life!

Many rural congregations will not be blessed with either of these options and may wonder if they can attempt anything with children. These congregations should look round at the range of gifts and skills that their members have amongst themselves. A quick survey will reveal a wealth of musical, physical and creative skills and interests that can be used to develop work with children and families. People who lack confidence to work with children in a traditional Sunday school setting may feel much more positive about leading an activity based on their hobby or passion. See the rest of this chapter for some ideas others have used successfully.

Starting work with children in your area

Despite the fact that children make up 20 per cent of the rural population, many churches consider that there are few children in their locality. Local church statistics show that over a quarter of rural Church of England churches have no children or young people attending their week by week services, compared with only 4 per cent of urban churches.[8]

The reality is more likely to be that children have no contact with the church – but are to be found in toddler and playgroups, pre-schools and schools, uniformed groups and wildlife clubs, musical gatherings and judo lessons.

One of the ways of finding out where the children in your community are, and what links with them already exist, is to conduct an audit or to draw up a parish profile. (Several books give good advice on how to do this – for example, see Margaret Withers, *Where are the Children?* – the details are in the Resources section.) Conducting such an audit exercise is a good way of identifying not just where the children are, but also highlighting any gaps in provision that the church may try to address. What do children and their families actually need? The audit may also reveal that church members are already involved in running groups and activities for children outside the church, which is a good way of building relationships. Some villages are 'twinned' with villages abroad – but are children included in the activities?

First suggestions

For example, sports facilities are rare in small villages but in some villages there may be a house with a swimming pool in the garden. If the owners are willing, opening the pool, with appropriate supervision, after school in the summer, even for just one day, could provide a valuable way of contacting families, creating a social occasion and even fund-raising for the church or a charity. If the pool could be made available on a regular weekly afternoon during the summer, this could be the beginning of a children's or families' group. Swimming, followed by a snack and a brief talk with perhaps an action song would be an excellent way of taking the gospel out into the community. A tennis court could be used in a similar way. One parish in Devon is investigating the possibility of marking out a badminton court (with the stained glass windows carefully shielded) inside the church when it is re-ordered.

Other rural communities will find other leisure possibilities to share. Dog walking is common, and it may be possible to organize a meeting time and place once a week so that children are welcome to walk their dogs in the company of two or more adults. This, too, could be followed by a snack (and a drink for the canine members of the group) if there is a welcoming home. (Do note, however, that even such an informal activity needs to be closely monitored by the church and child protection requirements strictly followed.)

Story: Sharing a passion

A woman in one Devon parish was passionate about sharing her love of the countryside. With encouragement from her church, and after appropriate CRB checks, she began a monthly group, with one other helper, for children to study wildlife in the field. She built good relationships with the children and gradually began to talk about the wonders of God's creation that she saw in the wildlife and the countryside. This approach could be adapted by anyone fascinated by archaeology, photography or the weather.

A practical activity such as the one described above could be developed like this:

- Find out whether such an activity is needed or would be welcomed by the local community (your audit should tell you this, or start asking people).

- Pray about and discuss the idea within the church.

- Funding and child protection issues need to be thought through and the activity will need to be formally noted and supported by the church council so that responsibility is fully shared by the church's leadership. Church members who decide to start an activity for children based on their own special interest, and any helpers, must undertake a CRB (Criminal Records Bureau) check and a risk assessment for the activity. They must be covered by the church's insurance, and parental consent forms should always be used. There is a helpful summary of all that is required in Margaret Withers' book, *Fired Up . . . Not Burnt Out* – details are in the Resources section.

- Identify two members of the congregation (or one with an interest and someone else prepared to support) who are willing to run the club.

- Find a venue. For example, you might approach the local school to offer to run a club as part of its 'extended school' programme. The school may already have the appropriate equipment and be glad to have someone to develop its use. If so, hold the club there. Otherwise, seek another suitable venue.

- Plan the activity: decide what equipment is needed, when you will meet and for how long. What would suit the local children?

- Advertise the club in the parish magazine, and put up posters in the health centre that serves the area, in the local school newsletter and anywhere else families from the village are likely to go, such as the pub. Make it clear in all publicity that the club is operated by a church group and that child protection guidelines will be rigorously followed.

- All enjoyable activities include refreshments so provide good-quality squash and biscuits. Hot chocolate would be popular in cold weather!

- At the end of each session, earth the activity in a Christian context, however simple. This can be something as simple as a prayer for the group or a short Scripture passage. For example, if you were running a 'weather club', you could point out that people have been fascinated by the weather for over 3,000 years and then read a different verse from the Bible at each session. The Psalms are a good source of weather references, but Jesus calming the storm, Elisha's servant looking for the cloud, and Paul's shipwreck would be interesting Bible stories to share once the children are comfortable with listening to the leaders.

- Explore whether the group's work can be posted on the Internet and help the children to visit good web sites on the subject if you can arrange even occasional access. Could another member of the congregation offer this once a month, or every three months?

- Be ready to adapt meetings to include events that link with the subject of the club. For example, if the topic was the weather, discuss any great weather events in the world such as hurricanes.

- Report back to the church regularly on progress. Consider having a special all-age service to celebrate the project. However, do not take it for granted that children from the club will attend (it can be too great a leap for some families at first). Just tell them that some of their activities are going to be shown to the Sunday congregation and invite them to come along with their families.

- Be encouraged! Even if only a few children come to the activity, this provides excellent opportunities to build relationships. For this sort of activity, small is indeed beautiful.

The subjects for such a club are limitless: here are a few suggestions but you will no doubt have your own, depending on what is needed in the local community and on what church members can offer:

astronomy	flower arranging
board games and/or chess	football
computer-based design	gardening
cooking	geology
crafts for Christmas or Easter	history
cycling proficiency	horses
embroidery	music
film-making	orienteering
fitness	singing

For ever and ever?

Many people have volunteered to help with children's work for a few weeks to fill a gap and have found themselves serving without a break for years and years. Club-based work need not be a life-sentence. A short course of perhaps just four meetings is manageable for the leaders and may be more attractive to children and their carers in busy lives. All the ideas mentioned above could be offered for a limited period. If the club goes well, and children are disappointed that it is coming to an end, a further series of meetings can always be offered later in the year.

What are churches trying to do?

Churches sometimes start working with children without deciding what they are actually trying to achieve. If the church leaders and those doing the children's work have not agreed on their aims, there are too many chances of disappointment with what does or does not come out of the activity. Many church members and leaders think that children's work is only of value if it results in children, and preferably their families too, attending Sunday services. This can lead to holiday clubs or fun days not being valued in themselves, but viewed only as a means of enticing unchurched families into 'proper' church. Holiday clubs must be valued for the ways in which they build relationships into the community and for their teaching element, which often plants valuable seeds of faith in those attending. They may reach many children. Such activities usually have a Christian theme so that children are learning about the gospel story.

Equally, activities that focus on sport or some local campaign such as helping to provide a playground for children are still evangelistic even though they may not include any Christian teaching. They are the church's witness in the community and should be prayed for and owned by the local church. However, church members will be disappointed if they think that investing time and effort in this way will encourage families to attend church.

Clear aims for any children's work will always avoid misunderstanding at a later date.

A case study: Handling a challenge

In one team of rural parishes, the priest's aim was to see children worshipping regularly at the Eucharist in the parish church. The organizers of the first steps towards working with children recognized that this aim was very long term, and that what they had in mind would be seen to have 'failed' if this was the only aim. Everyone, though, saw the possibilities for evangelism. After a long period of negotiation a series of ordered aims was identified:

- to make contact with a significant proportion of the children in the area in order to invite them to an outreach event with a Christian theme;
- to deliver the outreach event to such a high standard that children would want to return and their parents would be happy for them to do so;
- to repeat similar events in order to build up relationships and confidence on all sides;
- to review the pattern and nature of services within the team, looking carefully at how unchurched people, including children, and those on the fringe might be welcomed in church;
- to discuss within the parish the issue of administering communion before confirmation;
- to start inviting the families with whom good friendships have been formed to attend appropriate services at which they would not feel excluded;
- to welcome children and their families to worship at appropriate eucharistic services after careful preparation.

The overall aims of this outreach were clearly evangelistic, but, as can be seen above, after discussion they were broken down into smaller stepping stones. This meant that the children's workers did not get discouraged because they could not meet the priest's long-term aim immediately.

Moving about

> *There's no buses.* Owen, 7

Transport problems are at the heart of many rural issues. Few rural communities have regular bus services that enable older children, or young children brought by carers, to travel to clubs and events. Children are dependent on the goodwill or decision of adults, and the availability of a car. Churches do not always take responsibility for this. In one remote team of parishes, the Sunday school leader not only planned and delivered the programme to children but also drove round beforehand to collect them from the settlements where they lived and then drove them home afterwards. A single adult driving children alone is not good child protection practice. Other members of the church had no idea of the time and commitment involved, although they could easily have provided transport, and shared responsibility, on their way to worship. As is often the case, the church council needed to be aware of the work that was being done in its name, and to ensure that adequate support was given. All drivers providing transport should be accompanied by another adult, and both must have CRB clearance.

A story from Polzeath Family Mission, Cornwall

Polzeath Family Mission (PFM), sponsored by Scripture Union, has been operating at Polzeath beach for fifty years. Five years ago the outreach programme of PFM was extended so that all the local primary schools were visited in assembly to advertise the activities of the mission. It became obvious that children from one of the villages could not travel to attend the main mission as few of the families had access to transport. PFM leaders discussed the possibility of arranging transport for a group of these children to Polzeath. The challenges of finding a minibus, organizing insurance and providing team members to accompany the children seemed too great. After a year of reflection and prayer it was decided to repeat the main morning's activities from Polzeath at this village on four evenings during the period of the main mission. These repeat events in a church hall in the village were met with such enthusiasm that PFM decided to visit the village specially to run an evening event, in partnership with local children's workers, in each half-term.

Where to meet?

Meeting places can be difficult to find or reach. It is very difficult to run activities involving children in unheated, or ineffectively-heated, churches that lack kitchen and toilet facilities. Some churches have worked to adapt their building to create a warm welcome with suitable furniture and facilities, and meeting the needs of everyone, including those with disabilities. If it is not possible to do this with your church building or hall, it is better to seek out an alternative venue more suited to the purpose.

For example, one holiday club runs in a local bistro in the morning before the lunchtime rush – there are plenty of tables to work round and good loos, a kitchen to produce refreshments, and it is warm. This is a good example of making connections in a community. Others ask to use the primary school, perhaps before the school day starts, and may not have to pay. Some churches choose to hire the primary school for holiday or after-school club sessions to ensure a supply of chairs, tables and loos that are the right size for the children and access to a secure playground or field. Anglican churches may need only to pay for heating and caretaking if they book their local church school.

Questions for discussion

1. Where are the children in your community? What contacts do you already have? How could these be developed?

2. Is the church, or a hall, always the best place to work with children? Could you identify other suitable venues?

3. What interests do members of your church have that could be developed into a club with children?

2 Times and seasons

sharing the Church's year with the community,
and the community's year with the Church

*What I don't like about going to church is the readings are hard
to follow and understand.*

Lloyd, 9

In the past, the pattern of the church year closely mirrored the shape of the
agricultural year. Developments in agriculture mean that this is no longer true.
Harvest festivals are celebrated in September or October, but many children
living in the country know that oilseed rape is harvested in June, linseed and
winter barley in July and that few crops are gathered in during September.
The Church's year has not kept up with the changes in agriculture. As a
result, and perhaps contrary to the expectation of town dwellers, the points
of contact between what the Church is doing and what rural children are
experiencing in the year are few. In addition, few rural children live in families
where the main income comes from agriculture – either from working directly
on the land or in related service industries.

Although some children arrive at school having helped feed stock (and farm
families will be acutely aware if the weather is suitable for the hay harvest),
most rural children, like their urban cousins, will have barely noticed the
weather or the state of the fields. The need to connect children with the
pattern of agriculture can be just as great in rural areas as in the town, and
these traditional points in the Church's year can be used creatively to reach
out to children.

At the same time it should be remembered that rural children want to
celebrate the same events in the calendar as those who live in towns. New
Year, Red Nose Day, the Olympics and the World Cup, Mothering Sunday
and Father's Day, Children in Need and royal occasions all offer excellent
opportunities for churches either to join in events that the community is
planning or to take the lead in proposing a celebration. At the least these
will help develop relationships, but careful prayer and thought may provide
ways of sharing part of the gospel story.

The rest of this chapter contains practical suggestions for using the different times and seasons in the year to hold events or special services to reach out to children and families.

New Year

The New Year's Day bank holiday is a good time to organize a community event. Some churches organize a Christingle service for New Year to link with the festival of the 'Naming of Christ'. If children can make their own way to the venue, an event in the late morning would provide parents with the chance to recover from the previous evening's excitement, but an occasion open to all the family would also work well. An event that lasts about an hour and a half works well, though longer may be needed if a meal is to be shared.

Ideas for 'Gathering activities'

- A display board where people can write or draw anything they want to say thank you for that has happened in the previous year.
- Photographs from the previous year to enjoy, or a PowerPoint display of photographs. What were the highlights of life in the community over the past 12 months, good or bad?
- A large wastebin and pieces of newspaper and a sign inviting people to think of the things they regret in the previous year. They can either write on the paper or just think, before crumpling the paper and throwing it away.
- A giant calendar on which they can record the date of their birthday plus any special events that they have planned for the coming year.

Ideas for 'Getting-going' activities

- Asking everyone to line up in the order of their birthdays (less intrusive than lining up in order of age!) before singing Happy Birthday to the first person at the head of the line.
- An 'on this day' quiz to find out what special events and celebrity birthdays have happened on 1 January over the centuries.

Ideas for craft activities

● Making a calendar with a digital photo of the assembled company on it (use a digi-printer for instant photos). Provide a selection of Bible verses that can be glued onto the finished item.

● Planting single anemone corms in plastic pots or beakers of compost to take home.

● Creating a wall-painting or graffiti wall on wallpaper backing paper to show people's hopes and dreams for the year. This could be put on semi-permanent display in the village hall or church.

Ideas for games

● 'Birthday Bash' where different groups of people are called to the centre of the room, for example everyone born in January; everyone born on the 17th of any month; everyone born on the same date as someone else in their family.

● 'New from Old' – divide everyone into all-age groups of four or six; give them twelve sheets of newspaper, twelve empty yoghurt pots, and a roll of sticky tape, and give them ten minutes to make a hat for each person.

Ideas for Christian activities

● Singing 'Thank you, Lord, for this new year' (adapting words from *Junior Praise* 232).

● A two-minute talk on Hebrews 13.8, 'Jesus Christ is the same yesterday, today and for ever', or Ecclesiastes 3.1-8, pointing out that the new year will bring joys and sadness, but God remains constant.

● Telling the Creation story as presented by *Godly Play* to help everyone focus on the first beginning, and on the passage of time (for more information on *Godly Play*, see the Resources section at the end of the book).

Ideas for reflective activities

These can happen at the side of the room, for those of all ages who prefer not to be active.

- Comfortable chairs and beanbags with a selection of picture books and magazines to look at.
- Play-dough to work with.

Ideas for concluding activities

- Inviting everyone to write or draw one concern they have for the year ahead on a piece of card. The cards are pooled into a central box and then everyone draws out someone else's, which they take home. They are asked to pray over the days ahead for the request they have drawn.
- Provide an A5 sheet of card with the outline of the word 'peace' photocopied on it. Everyone decorates their card with pens, glitter or stickers. At the end of the event everyone swaps their peace card with someone else to 'exchange the peace'. Keen children will want to exchange their peace card with everyone there! Everyone takes home the card they are left with.
- Giving everyone a tealight candle to light from a central candle and challenging everyone to take theirs home without it going out. Explain they might want to think of the challenge of taking Jesus the Light of the World home with them for the new year.

Refreshments will depend on the time of day – coffee or juice and croissants would be good for a late morning slot; soup and rolls at lunchtime; tea and cake in the afternoon; a bring-and-share supper in the evening.

Epiphany

Some churches hold their Christingle service to coincide with Epiphany. Others take the opportunity for more carol-singing in the dark open air, by creating a costumed procession of wise people and pages. One parish did this as part of an Epiphany party with mulled fruit juice and mince pies, held in the church. They also discussed what presents they would have brought to offer baby Jesus, and made gift boxes to contain their ideas.

Wassailing

'Wassail', an old English word that is equivalent to 'Cheers!' or 'Good health', can be the starting point for another midwinter activity. Children love being out after dark. In one parish, the church and the school join together to enjoy a wassailing party. They go out into the local cider orchard with torches to ask God to bless the fruit trees. They sing 'Here we come a-wassailing' as they walk round the orchard before returning indoors for hot drinks and snacks. The whole community enjoys the event, and singing the carol with a chorus that asks God to bless the New Year makes it an event of outreach.

Plough Sunday

The second Sunday of January has been marked for centuries as Plough Sunday. It is a time to celebrate the long hours needed to prepare the soil before the seed can be sown. Of course many crops are now sown in the autumn to over winter but Plough Sunday is a good opportunity to mark the work of farmers.

Children enjoy seeing farm implements brought into church, such as a traditional plough, but modern equipment parked outside with the chance for children to sit in the cab would be fun.

Shrove Tuesday

Pancake Day receives much publicity in the media but it is not celebrated in all communities. If there is no local tradition of either making and eating pancakes, or racing with them, this is an easy custom to start. Offer to organize pancake races at the school or pre-school in a break or lunchtime, or straight after school. It may be possible to visit beforehand both to publicize the event and to explain about Shrove Tuesday being the last day before Lent and what that meant in the past about using up eggs. Remember that some people are allergic to eggs so identify an egg-free recipe for them.

Ash Wednesday

Giving up things for Lent is a strange idea for many people. It may be possible to organize an activity that starts discussion about consumerism or social justice. For example, a 'buy nothing day' arranged for Ash Wednesday would be a good starting point. Children love this kind of challenge. For further information on this, see the Resources section.

Holy Week

Many schools are on holiday during Holy Week so it can be a good time to run a holiday club or activity day. A 'Crafternoon' to make Easter decorations would be popular with children whilst providing an excellent occasion to tell the story of Easter and the meaning behind its customs.

Good Friday

Churches often choose to have quiet, reflective services on Good Friday that can exclude families. Parents worry that their children will disturb the calm atmosphere of Good Friday worship. Other churches choose to provide Good Friday workshops that meet the needs of children to be physically active and creative. Children may be invited to make the Easter Garden for display in the church, but with the stone carefully placed across the entrance to the tomb. (However, one church in Cumbria found that the children were much more interested in the ants that crawled out of the turf that had been brought in as the base of the garden, than in thinking about the story they were exploring!) Baking hot cross buns and explaining their symbolism is another way to share the significance of the day.

Easter

Older children might be delighted at the prospect of a sunrise breakfast. The top of a high hill in the area would make a great destination for a very early morning walk with the promise of a picnic on arrival. An Easter reading from one of the Gospels and a time of prayer would then be followed by everyone hurrying back home to share the good news of the resurrection. It might be possible to match the time of arrival back so that the children rush into the beginning of worship at the church with the good news.

In a small community, perhaps where few children have church links, it would be possible to deliver an Easter egg to the home of each child as a free gift with no expectation of a response. Of course, if a family service or an outreach activity is planned in the near future an invitation card could be attached to the box of the egg.

Rogation

Traditionally, Rogationtide, the days before Ascension Day, was the time for asking God's blessing on the fruits of the earth and the works of our hands. In the past, congregations would 'beat the bounds' by walking right round the boundaries of the parish. Many children would baulk at walking so far these days! Where churches are linked into a multi-parish benefice or with ecumenical partners it may be possible to hold a brief act of worship in one church before walking to another partner church where refreshments will be available. The walk could include simple enjoyment of the countryside, or it could take the form of a pilgrimage with various places (a farm, a workshop, a bridge, a ford or river, crossroads, a shop or pub) to visit to stop to pray for God's blessing.

Ascension

Coming 40 days after Easter Sunday, Ascensiontide is another opportunity to create a community event. As it happens on a Thursday, a school day, some churches invite their local school to ascend the church tower to look down on the local area. One primary school decided that only pupils in Year Six should be invited, making it the beginning of their school leavers' rituals. It is combined with a school Eucharist, and it has become a significant day in the school's calendar and pupils' lives whilst at the school.

Another team of parishes, with a significant geographical high point, developed a simple act of worship that involved walking up to the hilltop, reading from Acts 1, praying for the parishes they could see below, and then returning to share a meal in a local pub. Children loved the freedom of walking through the woods up to the high ground.

Midsummer

Fetes and fundraising events abound in the middle of summer. See Chapter 4, 'Belonging and being', for ideas to reach children at these events. Some communities have reinvented old customs or created new traditions to make the most of warmer days and lighter evenings.

Two villages, just over a mile apart across the fields, planned to hold a 'revel' to mark the millennium. The organizing committee raised money in different ways to fund creative workshops in the run-up to May Day. The first time the revel was held everyone decided it had been a lot of work but enormous fun. Everyone walked, carrying a huge wooden arrow, made previously, from one village to the second, where there were maypole dancing, drama and sports activities. The churches as institutions did not get involved. When it was decided to repeat the day, two years later after all threat of foot-and-mouth disease had lifted, the church offered to welcome everyone to a brief service of sending-out before they set off across the fields to the next village. The offer was welcomed and the church was filled to capacity at the start of a great community day. Many of the children present had only previously been to the church with the school. The day has become established as a new tradition and the churches have secured their role within it. This opportunity could easily have been missed.

Harvest

Most churches celebrate their harvest thanksgiving between the middle of September and early October. Even in rural areas, attendance has often declined at these services in recent years as churches have not held their place at the heart of the community. Some churches have understood that if families are not coming along to a traditional service, then other forms of service and thanksgiving need to be explored. Even if it is decided to keep to a traditional service, there are plenty of ways to reach out to children and their families at harvest time. A fairly wide idea of harvest and thanksgiving will produce the best response.

- Put a leaflet advertising the Harvest Thanksgiving through each letterbox in the village. Add a tear-off slip asking for suggestions of what people would like to give thanks for. Even one reply is of value.

- The request could be put in the village magazine or even publicized through the local paper by contacting the news desk with a story headed 'Local Church Wants to say Thanks!'

- Develop this idea by escorting older children to knock on doors to ask for ideas to include in the thanksgiving service. Make sure all suggestions are included.

- Invite children at the local school or uniformed organization to write or draw what they would say thank you for. If there is no school or group, contact the children with a personalized letter to ask for contributions. This could take the form of a competition with small prizes of a Christian book for all entrants.

- Ask children to help decorate the church for the thanksgiving. One parish did this and was delighted by a display of toy tractors and a model farm.

- Organize simple sports or games in the church or churchyard before the harvest service, and serve refreshments. Some families will stay for the service.

- A harvest meal at lunchtime or the early evening (bring-and-share in the hall; provided by church members; or a simple flat-price menu at the pub) can be a good gathering point. The briefest of humorous talks or a slightly extended grace may be all that is required to share something of the gospel.

The Feast of St Francis

Some churches have started to hold a service of blessing for animals around 4 October, to link with St Francis' Day. Pets can be brought to church, with the smaller ones invited inside. Alternatively, a similar service could be held in a field with a selection of farm animals, suitably penned, alongside pets. Even in country areas, some children get little opportunity to meet a sheep or cow face to face. If children are allowed to handle the animals, provide moist wipes so that they can clean their hands afterwards. Outdoor worship always feels different, and this could easily become an annual tradition. A pet or animal service does not have to be limited to St Francis' Day, when it may be too close to harvest celebrations. A late spring or summer date may suit the community better.

Apple Day

The idea of buying local foods where possible, and the importance of preserving traditional varieties, have encouraged the development of a national Apple Day in October. Churches could develop an event to link with this both to support local growers and to connect with children in the community.

Activities might include:

- apple dunking;
- tasting segments of different apples and juices to try to guess the varieties;
- making apple prints by cutting apples in half vertically, to show the star formed by the core, and then dipping the halves into paint;
- creating a mural with the outline of an apple tree's trunk and branches and inviting everyone to cut out an apple shape on which they can write their name and then glue to the 'tree';
- learning the carol 'Jesus Christ the Apple Tree'.

In farming areas it can be important to champion the purchase of locally-produced food. Should a church buy the cheapest food to put on a meal, or spend more money to support local farmers?

All Saints and All Souls

Unlike those in urban areas, many village churchyards are still open for new burials, so children may have a connection with a grave there. Older children could be invited to help tidy the churchyard ready for the season of remembrance. A special event could arranged for the nearest weekend with children (indeed, everyone) invited to make a posy of flowers from a selection provided by the church to lay on either their special grave, or on a grave that is unlikely to be visited. At an advertised time, brief prayers of remembrance and an appropriate song could be sung out in the churchyard, although the church could be used if the weather is poor. The Register of Burials could be on display so that families could look up details of the person they are remembering. The Baptism Register could also be on display to emphasize that God plays a part in all ages and aspects of life.

Some communities have started an annual 'Lantern Procession' that takes place once the clocks have gone back to Greenwich Mean Time. Beautiful 3-D models made of withies (willow twigs) and tissue paper, and illuminated internally by battery-powered bulbs, are made in workshops in the run-up to the event and then carried in procession. Churches could get involved with events already happening by creating their own large-scale lantern, or they could start such an event as a way of linking with the community.

Christmas

Christmas celebrations are many and various in rural areas, and some villages have difficulty in finding enough evenings to fit in all the events. The weeks leading up to Christmas Day provide many opportunities for the church to reach out to the children at a time when families are happy to include religious reflection in the midst of all the preparations. Many rural churches recognize that attendance by children goes up in November and December, only to fall away again in January when it seems that people feel they have 'done' religion for a while. This means that churches need to make the most of this period of openness.

Ways of reaching out to children at Christmas might include:

- Using the Mexican tradition of 'Posada', as it has been adapted to European village life. This offers an opportunity to re-enact the struggle of Joseph and Mary to find a room for the night when they went to Bethlehem. Different families around the community offer to take figures of Joseph and Mary home for the night. A special prayer can be said as each family hands on the responsibility, and families may decide to share a special meal or carol sing-a-long with friends as they play host. Fuller details can be obtained from the Church Army; alternatively, there is a version in the CHP resource *Together for a Season* (see the Resources section for both of these).

- Offering to provide refreshments at the school's carol service, or nativity or other Christmas play. This provides an opportunity to build relationships with children and their families.

- Inviting children to assemble the church crib, even if no crib service is planned. This gives an opportunity to explain the purpose of the nativity scene. One church, needing to replace its crib figures, invited three boys from the village to travel to the nearest city to help in their selection.

- Inviting everyone to come to church dressed as their favourite nativity character to create a 'Nativity from Scratch'. Any number of angels, shepherds and kings can be accommodated but a flexible script is needed in case you have to cope with several Marys! For example, the narrator could point out that everyone is called to welcome Jesus into their life just as Mary did, and it is good to see so many happy to do that on this occasion. A good mix of traditional carols and Christmas songs that children have learned at school will ensure everyone has a happy experience of being in church.

● Organizing a 'Carols of Praise' works well in a small community, as those selected to choose a carol and to talk about their choice will be well known. It is good to include children in this, even if a parent has to explain their choice, as it will ensure that music enjoyed by their age group is included.

A story from St Giles, Lea, Wiltshire

Christmas Eve was chosen as the best time to stage a live nativity in a barn in the centre of the village. The events started at the church with Caesar Augustus issuing a decree that a census should be taken of the entire Roman Empire, and that everybody should go to their home town to be registered. Mary and Joseph were in the church. Everyone then set off through the village knocking on doors to see if anyone had room for Mary and Joseph to stay. When everyone got to the barn, they met a kind innkeeper who let them use the stable for the night. The cast continued to act out the story, with a baby being placed in the manger, and carols being sung to fit in with the events.

Many people chose to take part in this and many said it was the most meaningful Christmas service that they had been to. Everyone shared refreshments at the end.

Questions for discussion

1. What are the highlights of the year in your community? Is the church involved with them? If not, are there opportunities for this to develop?

2. Does it matter that the church year has few links with the farming, school or national calendar?

3. When are the quiet times of year in your community? What event or activity could you hold then to reach out to children and their families?

3 Rites of passage

reaching children and their families at significant moments in their lives

There aren't very many children my age, and although that's good sometimes, other times it is a little dull.

Lucy, 11

The circle of life

The traditional role of the village church in 'hatching, matching and despatching' parishioners has changed significantly over the past quarter of a century. Many churches report that often the first contact they have with a family is when they ask for their baby to be baptized. The parents may not be married, and they regard the baptism as a public statement and celebration that they are a family. In other instances, couples decide to get married and have their child baptized at the same ceremony, or they choose to have their civil marriage blessed in the same service as the baptism. In choosing to organize the service in this way, the couple may be indicating that they would prefer a more informal, child-friendly approach. This requires churches to be much more flexible both in their outreach and in what they offer within the service.

Children are often present at baptisms, weddings and blessings, and, less often, funerals. It may be a rare, or even first, visit to church for a service. The welcome and experience they receive may have far-reaching consequences. Some churches may feel that there is little point in reaching out to visiting children whom they will probably never see again but others are happy to sow seeds that other churches may be privileged to reap. Here are some ways you can welcome children at these occasions:

- Provide an activity sheet about baptism or marriage, with things to do such as a wordsearch or maze, a relevant picture to colour in, a memory verse, and so on. Once these have been created, fresh copies can be produced for each occasion. Make sure that there are plentiful supplies of colouring pens that work for older children, and thick crayons for the youngest, at the back of the church.

- Provide an activity bag, which could include sheets to colour, and relevant books, such as *My Baptism Book*, or the *Baptism Cube* (see Resources list).

- Provide a reflective space for children to withdraw to during the service. Make sure that the minister points it out in the welcoming remarks. Beanbags or large cushions are good for children of all sizes, but their carer might prefer a proper chair if they are dressed for a family celebration. Provide a range of Bible picture books and storybooks for all ages, rather than the familiar secular books that children see in school or in the doctor's waiting room. Soft toys to cuddle would also be a good idea, but avoid anything that will make a noise as it is played with or dropped. These toys should be as new, clean and attractive as possible.

- At a baptism, invite children to come close to the font so they can see what is happening, and ask brothers and sisters, or cousins, to hold the minister's book or the napkin so they are able to play a real part in the proceedings.

- Discuss with couples considering a wedding or a wedding blessing, especially those celebrating a second marriage, if they have children and whether they would like to involve them in the service or have them close by.

- Churches could ensure that there is a selection of clean, welcoming children's books, including some that deal with bereavement and loss, for children to look at when attending a funeral. A sidesperson should be ready to point out the book corner to visiting children, as they may be too awed or upset to explore themselves. Suggestions for suitable books are included in the Resources section.

Another way to ensure that children are fully involved in the occasion would be to arrange a prayer encounter that picks up the theme of the sermon and the occasion. Here are some ideas for this:

- Give everyone a small square of paper on which they are invited to write or draw a prayer for the child being baptized or the couple being married or blessed. Children could gather up the prayers in baskets so the minister could offer them to God. A member of the congregation could then later paste them into a presentation book to give to the family as a keepsake. This would then form part of the follow-up.

- At a wedding or blessing, give everyone a short length of string or ribbon (this could coordinate with the colour scheme of the couple!). Ask everyone to pray for the couple as they tie a single knot in their string; then to pray for all who will support the couple in their life together, as they tie a second knot; and then to pray that everyone will be faithful in their relationships just as Jesus was faithful to his Father, as they tie a third knot. Children could be invited to gather up the knotted strings or ribbons in baskets so all the prayers can be presented at the altar. Again, a member of the congregation could join all the strings or prayers into a long line to present to the couple as part of the follow-up.

- The water theme of the baptism service could be developed by using bubbles for the prayers. Explain that everyone is invited to pray about each bidding as long as they can see bubbles floating in the air. Invite one child to be ready to blow bubbles from a small pot when given a signal (two or three children might be needed if the congregation is large). The first section of prayer is read, the signal is given and the bubbles are blown. Once all the bubbles have disappeared, repeat with the next bidding. Small pots of bubbles are the cheapest and simplest way of doing this, but battery-powered bubble blowers can be bought from toy shops for a more spectacular effect.

The other end of life

Funerals pose greater difficulties for involving children. There is still a trend in the UK for children to be kept away from funerals and, in rural life, where the turnout is often great, this means that they are absent from what can be important community gatherings. Church members responsible for helping families make funeral arrangements can emphasize that children are welcome at the service and need not be excluded. Parents and carers may need to be encouraged to give children the option to attend.

Many people, of whatever age, are likely to be distressed or uncomfortable, so church members must work sensitively to help them feel at ease. The reflective children's space described above could be adapted to include a large sand-tray (or a low table with several small trays of sand) for children to sift during the service. Playing with sand is very therapeutic. A member of the congregation could sit alongside to supervise and provide gentle, prayerful support.

At the same time, churches may wish to prepare a booklet of ideas to give to children to help them to express their feelings of loss through drawing pictures, writing stories or prayers, or creating a memory box. This will involve children in the grieving process even if they do not come to church.

Following up

Many churches send anniversary cards to children who have been baptized in their church. However, many decide to stop doing so after the child is five years old, particularly if the family has not been seen back in church. To stop then is illogical, for that is just the age when a child may appreciate the arrival of a special card. Until that age, the card is really for the parents! Churches serious about building relationships with children and their families will continue to send baptism anniversary cards until the child has become adult or even until the church loses contact with them. After all, the church makes promises at the baptism as well as the parents and godparents. There are comparatively fewer baptisms in rural parishes so the task should be more manageable.

Parents and carers at home with small children have few places where they can 'drop in'. Churches can be inventive in their response to these needs.

One team of churches decided to copy the story-and-activity sessions offered by a town library, in church. A monthly 'Storytime' session was organized with a gathering activity so that children had something to do as soon as they arrived, an introduction to the session's theme using a treasure box for the children to find and open, a Bible story, a related craft activity, a 'thank you' song, a brief time of reflection around a candle, and refreshments. All this fitted into just over half an hour. The session was timed so that parents could go straight on to collect older children from school. Storytime worked well for about a year until the group of children attending started school. It proved difficult to make links with the next cohort. The leaders decided to move the event to another village where the pre-school was keen to use it as an outing within the community. Themes used for these sessions included 'The Lost Sheep', 'Weather' and 'The Lost Coin', with a special nativity afternoon in December.

The difficulties posed by cold church buildings in the winter, and poor facilities, might prompt you to arrange such events in a home. Occasionally schools may have a spare classroom or hall available for part of the day that could be used. Many schools recognize the value of good links with the community and the need for small children to have the chance to develop their communication skills. This means that schools may not make a charge to use their facilities. Good relationships at all levels can produce results.

A Story from Great Bentley, Essex

Tiny children in the village are each given a teddy bear hand-knitted by members of the church, and invited to bring it along to 'Bentley Bears'. When they arrive in the church each month, there is a story from the Teddy Horsley series, prayer and lots of songs. Children are given percussion instruments to play. Everyone then moves into the carpeted meeting room where children can play with toys whilst refreshments are served. Everything finishes in time for parents to collect older children from the primary school. In this parish, Bentley Bears provides a way in to the life of the church. It is part of a wider pattern of family-friendly church life, which includes regular all-age worship, a Sunday school and a weekly after-school club. Children moving on from Bentley Bears are encouraged to join the next appropriate activity.

Pinch points

All children face challenges when they move on to the next phase of life, particularly when they start or change school. For children living in scattered or isolated settlements, the feelings of challenge, and even abandonment, when they know that they cannot just walk home, can be much greater.

Some churches choose to work with children, and their families, at these pinch points to offer support and encouragement. A number of resources are available to help in this task (see the Resources list for more details). *Get Ready Go* by Margery Francis was written to help small children as they start school for the first time. It can be bought and given to each child moving on from playgroup, pre-school or nursery. A special party could be held, perhaps at the pre-school if this can be negotiated, when the books are given out and the children prayed for. It may take a number of months to build up a relationship so that this is possible, but one church member regularly visiting the group, even just to do some washing up, can bring about great change in relationships. Work with the under-fives may be the most fruitful way for a rural church to develop friendships and outreach.

The *Storykeepers* initiative (contact details are in the Resources section) is a good way of linking with children, aged about seven, as they move to junior school, or on to Key Stage 2. The scheme provides a presentation pack with a DVD with two *Storykeepers* episodes that tell stories about Jesus in cartoon form, along with a game and a sheet of stickers. Research has shown that children will happily watch the same cartoon or programme over and over with great satisfaction until they are eight. At this point they prefer to watch new material or to pursue a range of other activities. So age six or seven is a good time to give them a DVD or video that can be watched many times. The presentation pack can be given to all the children of that age group in the local school or village. After a month, the children are invited to a *Storykeepers* party where another episode is shown. Material from the *Storykeepers* initiative gives clear guidance on how to organize this outreach, including exactly how to run the party. The small numbers involved in rural areas makes this an effective way to reach out to children.

The move on to secondary school is particularly difficult for children in rural areas. If they have been used to a five-minute walk to primary school, they may now find they face an hour on a bus to get to secondary school. They may be transferring with only one or two others from their village class. The Scripture Union publication, *It's Your Move!* (see Resources section) provides excellent advice for youngsters and it has been used creatively by many churches.

Losing touch

I like the Youth Exchange services best. Simon, 12 (these
services are planned by and for older children and teenagers)

In some rural areas, nearly all the children from a primary school move on
together into the same secondary school. In other areas the cohort is split
up and ministers may not be able to maintain contact with them. Some rural
deaneries have addressed this problem by employing a deanery-based
worker to work with children between the ages of ten and fourteen to build
relationships and to try to achieve continuity. Such workers provide stability
for the children when some of their pastoral support is changing. Deaneries
or circuits that do not employ a worker would do well to review the provision
they make for older children as they move into their teens. Some secondary
schools welcome visitors to run lunchtime Christian clubs and parishes could
work together to do this.

The big wide world

Children from affluent rural homes will be given many opportunities to
experience the wider world through holidays and family activities. Pony
Club gymkhanas and camps, and the junior clubs affiliated to organizations
such as the National Federation of Young Farmers and the Royal Society
of Wildlife Trusts provide children with the chance to pursue countryside
interests on a wider scale.

However, children from poorer homes have far fewer opportunities to
broaden their horizons. One school, an hour from the nearest small city,
identified that some of its pupils had never ridden on an escalator or in a lift,
nor looked down on life from anything higher than the first floor. The local
church helped organize a day trip to the city so that the children could travel
up to the fifth floor of a department store to observe people walking along
the high street below. This church grasped the possibilities of helping the
children in its area to experience life in all its fullness. It was a very small act
of outreach but it made a real difference to some of those children. This is
not an isolated problem. Many children only travel between home and
school and doctor's outpost surgery, and may never visit a town.

Questions for discussion

1. What provision does your church make for children at baptisms, weddings and funerals? If this is a rare event for them, what will they have gained from experiencing worship with you?

2. How do children in your community know that they are valued by the church? Are there occasions in their lives when the church can provide support and help?

3. How can you help children to experience more of the world around them?

4 Belonging and being

the Church as both gathering point and contributing partner in the community

I don't go to church. Lucy, 11

In a village, you know everybody. Lloyd, 9

Who belongs?

Is it possible, in a village, to answer the question 'who belongs to the church?' Is it the parents who are on the electoral roll? All those who are baptized? All who attend, however irregularly, across the year? Are children members in their own right? A rural church is rarely a 'gathered' congregation in the way that many suburban churches are. It is much more the symbol of the presence of Christ at the centre of a community.

Some rural parishes report that the number of baptisms remains the same as in the 1980s, whilst others describe a falling-off similar to that experienced in urban areas. Some country parishes work hard to maintain contact with the children they have baptized, ensuring that they receive personal invitations to family services and other church events. Research shows that the more open the baptism policy of a rural church, the larger its standard Sunday congregation is likely to be.[1] This link does not hold true for urban and suburban churches.

There would appear to be far greater affinity with the building, and even what goes on inside it, in rural places among people who rarely attend, than in larger towns. At the same time it is impossible to say with confidence that people who move into a village, 'incomers', are more likely to be active in children's work and evangelism than those who are long-term residents or who were born in the village. There is no clear pattern.

A feature of many villages is the rise in the number of properties that are second homes. When they remain empty for long periods of time, such houses can feel like a drain on the community. When they are used by families keen to join in village life, they can be a blessing of refreshment. Some churches plan to hold child-friendly services to coincide with holiday weekends when they are sure that occasional residents will be around. Many people who buy a second home want to feel part of the community they visit, and attending church can be a good way to build relationships.

The church can be a gathering point for the community where long-term residents, incomers and second-home visitors come together. Congregations may have to work deliberately to foster this sense of community both through opportunities at services and by providing occasions for people to come together. Children love to feel that they belong.

Gathering activities are popular. They provide something to do as soon as children arrive at the worship or activity venue. Children soon learn that the interest and involvement will start straight away and can be seen to run to take part. Where parents have been asked to help lead this activity, they prefer not to be right at the front; where leaders are involved, it is good to have the activity where everyone can see what is going on. This reflects the differing levels of confidence of those leading such an activity. If parents do not feel comfortable, however much they value the activity, they will refuse to take part.

Building relationships within a community

Relationships are the key feature of all effective evangelism. One of the strengths of village life is that children are often well known and it is easy to identify where they live so they can receive personal invitations. Church members are likely to meet the same children and families at a range of activities: shopping, visiting the doctor, school events or community celebrations. Some churches use their relationships well to work creatively with a community's desire to get together. Planned effectively, collaboration with the community can provide much encouragement for a church. As ever, careful focus on the aims of the collaboration makes sure that everyone is happy with both the effort and the outcome.

A story from Chawleigh, Devon

The church wanted to run a holiday club but realized that there were too few of them to be able to run it effectively. So they came up with the idea of inviting the community to help run a village holiday club with a Christian basis. The community was easily persuaded that it would be fun to come together during the summer as the lack of activities had already been identified. They chose an overall theme of 'Tree-mendous' and included a drama about Zacchaeus, a nature trail and sports. The event ran for four days, spilling over into the Sunday service, and attracted nearly half the children in the small village school. Such a good proportion of the teenagers and adults in the village contributed and took part that it could be described as an all-age holiday club. People of all ages led sessions based on their interests and talents. When the club was reviewed later in the year, the large leadership team emphasized the importance of hospitality – they felt the effort they had put into welcoming people and providing refreshments was a key part of their success. The review also recognized the need to provide extra social time as everyone wanted more time to chat and be together. They were identifying the lack of opportunities for people to come together in the village. One leader, reflecting on the needs of local children, considered that cycling proficiency should be included in a future event.

Many churches have learned that the most effective way to work with children is by running a series of linked events so that relationships can be fostered. The most difficult part is making the initial contact, but once children have attended something they have enjoyed, it is then much easier to invite them to the next event. Plans for this event need to be in place therefore, so that the next event is already in the pipeline for children to be told about it. For example, one Devon parish invited families to a crib service, then to a Christingle party and then to the first ever family service. The new family service became quickly established.

More than a holiday club

Some churches, or groups of churches (either from a team of parishes, but more usually from different denominations), cooperate to put on full missions to reach out to local children. Whilst holiday clubs usually operate for a couple of hours each day for a week, missions tend to offer a much wider programme, often for up to a fortnight. Many operate in seaside places and appeal to visitors as well as resident families. There are a few that are firmly rooted in a village. The volume of activity and the amount of planning required mean that such missions are rare. One or two have developed as 'satellites' of larger events, recognizing that it is difficult for children to travel to them. One village mission in the north-east decided to use a minibus to transport children to a larger event when it could not find enough volunteers to run its own. In some instances, overall leaders are recruited from outside to head up events run by local people.

What next?

Sometimes churches are puzzled that families who have attended a holiday club enthusiastically do not always start coming to church. There are two main reasons for this. The first is that families may have used the holiday club as inexpensive childcare. They have been delighted by the church's offering of service to them and their children. They are not looking for any further involvement than that. In this instance, the church must be happy to have had the opportunity to serve its community and, possibly, to have planted some seeds of faith and shared some of the gospel story with the children.

The second reason is that the church service to which families are invited at the end of the holiday club frequently bears little resemblance to the club sessions that have been greatly enjoyed. Holiday clubs rarely expect children to sit down for more than five minutes at a time. They include an enjoyable mix of crafts, games, teaching, refreshments, activity and sometimes worship. They take place in a hall where children are not expected to sit quietly and reverently.

Churches that seek to build a new congregation through a holiday club need to plan a regular 'holiday club church service' to meet the needs of those children and their families, rather than trying to squeeze them into a slightly-adapted version of a service that already exists.

A story from Calthwaite, Cumbria

Sunday was not the right day to run a children's club for 5–11-year-olds, so the Rainbow Club has been moved to the Saturday afternoon before the monthly Family Communion the following day. The club frequently includes a *Godly Play* story, and always features a *Godly Play* 'Feast'. The use of the *Godly Play* 'Feast' makes very good links with the service of Holy Communion. At the club, children are allocated tasks to undertake at the service the next day. Ringing the bell is particularly popular, but they also give out books, take up the elements for the Communion and the older ones may be asked to read a lesson. Some 15 children attend the club and a handful of families come to the Family Communion, with many more for special occasions. The confirmation class also makes use of *Godly Play* in its preparation.

The parish also runs an activity day in the local primary school, which attracts some 35 children during Holy Week. This sometimes includes sharing a Passover Meal. Good Friday is marked by a three-mile walk, following a portable cross, along the back lanes to the largest church in the benefice for a service.

Parents have been gradually drawn into the church's activities, so that now the church is mainly run by people in their forties, although the church officers are older.

(Details of *Godly Play* can be found in the Resources section.)

Living stones

Many rural churches are open during daylight hours and often receive a surprising number of visits across the week. However, prayer boards and guides to the building are usually directed at adults. There is little provision to engage a visiting child. Some churches create displays, perhaps using newspaper reports, as a prayer focus at times of disaster, such as the death of Princess Diana, 9/11 or the Asian tsunami. These are good as far as they go, but often fail to consider whether a child would be interested in the display or even able to see it physically.

- A prayer encounter such as post-its to write or draw on before being attached to a cross; tealight candles to light from a central candle, in front of a poster of 'The Light of the World'; a chance to draw themselves on a small piece of paper to be stuck onto a larger display where everyone will be prayed for.

- Christian entertainment such as puppets miming to songs, a clown or storyteller, an illusionist or face-painter will all hold children's attention.

- A scrolling display of images to illustrate, for example, the words of a Psalm or Genesis 1 will attract many children to gather around a laptop computer to watch and reflect.

A stand at an event is unlikely to bring a child to faith. There will be insufficient time for a relationship to be built. However, the stand may send out a strong message that local Christians enjoy having fun, and that they want to share their faith with children. It will raise the profile of the local church(es) with both parents and children, and it may sow seeds for a child or awaken the interest of a family. At the very least, no one will be able to say that the church is not interested in anything other than itself!

Questions for discussion

1. Whom do you regard as members of your church? How is membership decided? Would your community agree with your answers?

2. Do the people you regard as church members match the age range of your community?

3. Does your church building speak to visitors, especially children, if they drop in? Do you need to make any changes?

4. What local events take place where you could organize an outreach stand for children?

Ideas for reaching out to children visiting your church

- Provide a children's corner with Christian books to look at. Some churches change what they provide for children according to the liturgical season, using an appropriately coloured cloth, books that link with the time of year, and activity sheets and pens.

- Invite children to write or draw prayers for a prayer board displayed at their height.

- A prayer encounter that encourages children to light a candle in prayer, to listen to the sounds within themselves, the building and beyond, or to add their self-portrait to a picture of people being prayed for.

- A simple guide to the main features of the church explaining how they are used. This could be a take-home activity sheet that children could follow like a treasure trail.

The village school could be invited to visit the church and then to write a guidebook for visiting children, or to suggest activities that children might enjoy when looking around. This could be part of a Design Technology project for junior pupils.

Twinning

Many villages are 'twinned' with villages across the world, and twinning organizations offer many opportunities for outreach. The nature of the links varies and a congregation needs to listen carefully to identify ways of getting involved. It may be that the involvement of children is very limited, and the church could find a way of helping them take part fully.

One church provided space for the village school to put on an exhibition about its links around the world. Flags from all the countries that individual pupils had visited or where they had email links were hung from the roof, emailed pictures and letters from partnered schools were displayed on boards, and a special assembly was held in church to highlight the idea that everyone lives in a global village. The school was delighted to have access to a large display space, and the church built good relationships through the warm welcome it offered.

Let's do the show right here!

Agricultural and country shows are popular in rural areas. The big agricultural shows around the country often have Christian welcoming stands and displays. These are usually organized by the appropriate branch of Churches Together. Activities for children, including quizzes, free refreshments and bouncy castles, extend a positive welcome to families and youngsters. It would be interesting to analyse how many of those visiting the stand already have some level of faith or church connection. Setting up attractive activities for children, such as face-painting, right at the entrance to the stand could provide a chance to make contact with families without expecting them to enter what may be perceived as 'Church' and, therefore, threatening space. If positive conversations ensue, then they can be encouraged to enjoy refreshments or to look around further.

Local country shows, ploughing matches, steam rallies, car boot sales and garden club competitions provide excellent opportunities for churches to reach out to children. The size of the event determines how much a pitch or stand will cost. Some village-based shows are happy to provide a vacant slot for free, leaving the church to organize its own tent. One small rural team provided its own tent, table and chairs so that the only costs incurred were the cost of admission for those staffing the stand.

Larger events will make a charge for a pitch and may provide space within a large marquee. This would be a good opportunity for a deanery, a circuit or a Churches Together group to work in partnership. Careful budgeting and requests for the donation of materials will keep costs to a manageable level. However a 'make-do-and-mend' approach will be counter-productive. Funding may be required if you decide that you want to provide give-away gifts or resources on the stand of the same quality as those offered by trade stands.

A church stand should be attractive to children. This may seem obvious, but many outreach activities lack 'eye-appeal' to children. Borrowing colourful plastic chairs and tables from a nursery for toddlers to gather round, and larger ones from a school for older children, to set out at the entrance will make a good start on this. Brightly-coloured balloons and coloured fairy lights, if there is access to electricity or a suitable battery, help to attract attention. Helpers could wear bright, matching T-shirts with a logo to identify them both on the stand and as they walk round the showground.

A banner, flag or a static kite with the same logo could also be used. Obviously banners and T-shirts could be used for more than one year to keep costs down. Parents may appreciate knowing who is sponsoring the activity but these details can be displayed inside the tent. The children will either see something that catches their attention – and make a bee-line for it – or they will wander on by to something else that looks fun.

The activities offered will be determined by the aims of taking a stand at the show. There is little to be gained from offering bouncy castles if there a commercial or charity stands doing the same – indeed their organizers ma be unhappy to have their income reduced! If churches are going to under the effort of organizing a stand, the purpose must be to provide children v an opportunity to experience God and to learn something about the Chris faith. A range of activities to meet the needs of different age groups and those with special needs should be devised. An overall theme, perhaps linking in with the theme of the show or event, would help focus the decorations and the choice of activities. The following are some suggestio

- For the smallest children: colouring sheets, play dough, sand trays and soft toys.

- For older children: quizzes, with the answers to be found from a display, and a small prize for every child who has a go.

- To give away: freebies, such as a pencil or rubber with a Bible verse, tiny Christian books and badges (which could be hidden in a bran tu Sweets have no 'teaching' purpose, and will be given away at commercial stands anyway, so you may not want to go for this optio

- Have a huge container of coloured pipe-cleaners and invite children to sculpt their image of God.

- Pebble painting provides an opportunity for people of all ages to sit and chat amid the hectic activity of a show. Provide a heap of smoo stones, available from garden centres, and marker pens or acrylic paints for people to use. Suitable Bible texts to display around this creative activity might include 1 Chronicles 29.8; Ecclesiastes 3.5; Matthew 3.8-9; 1 Peter 2.4-6.

Helium-filled balloons on which children are invited to write or draw prayer with felt-tip pens before they are released (this may not be permitted at ag ultural shows because of the danger that deflated balloons can pose to anima

5 Encouragement from a small Devon parish

I like living in a village because it's quiet and pretty. You know everybody. It's nice that you can go for walks without going in the car first (that means you can have a dog). Lloyd, 9

Brampford Speke is a small village with some 350 residents just four miles north of Exeter in Devon. There is a Church of England Voluntary Controlled School with around 55 pupils, drawn from the village, the neighbouring village and the fringes of Exeter. The shop closed a decade ago, but the pub has reopened after a decade of being shut. There are several working farms in the parish, but most have given up dairy work so that cattle and sheep are no longer herded along the main lane. The number of people working on the land has declined and many more people commute to Exeter. St Peter's church was rebuilt in the 1850s and has changed little in layout since.

The last resident vicar retired in 1982 so the parish has found itself in a gradually expanding team – first of four, then five and now eight parishes with eleven churches – looked after by a priest-in-charge who lives in the next, and larger, village.

Throughout all these changes, considerable efforts had been made to keep children's work going. Twice-monthly lay-led family services were held and attendance was often close to 40. Involvement in these services led to two leaders training as lay readers. Specially-written Christmas plays provided much excitement over five years and holiday club afternoons were held weekly during the summer holidays for several years. But children's work wound down as the children in the village grew older and stopped taking part. The family services came to an end, apart from four special occasions to mark Mothering Sunday, St Peter's Week, a Christingle or other charity-focused service in Advent, and Christmas morning.

In the late 1990s the make-up of the village changed. A number of families with babies and very young children moved in. Several asked for their babies to be baptized and enquired about the provision the church made to work with children. This request was made both to the priest-in-charge and to the pre-school leader who was known as a church member. The level of interest inspired one of the lay readers in 2001 to propose a monthly family service that would focus specifically on the needs of children under eight and their families. A very tight specification was drawn up for the service:

- it should last only 35 minutes;

- it needed a sharp name that could develop the feel of a brand; it was named 'Service with a Smile ☺';

- there should be a gathering activity to interest children as soon as they arrived in church;

- there should be a story slot illustrating the day's theme aimed at the smallest children, who would be sitting on a rug by the chancel step;

- there should be good quality refreshments;

- the range of music would include a traditional hymn, and a song with actions or simple, repetitive chorus;

- active prayers would alternate monthly with formal prayers;

- the theme would follow closely the lectionary readings used by the other parishes of the benefice;

- visual displays and physical activity were to be included whenever possible.

These aims were shared as widely as possible through the parish magazine, advertising fliers delivered through the school, pre-school and letterboxes, and by word of mouth.

'Service with a Smile ☺' was launched with a harvest theme in September 2001. The first service attracted 48 people, including 21 children. After nearly five years, the average attendance has grown from 33 in 2002 to 45 in 2005. The congregation includes not just the young families for whom it was founded and designed, but many retired people, both local and from surrounding villages. Graffiti-style comment sheets have been used occasionally to find out what those attending think about the service. These are extremely positive and highlight the cheerful informality, the warm relationships and the good provision for small children. They are less positive about the absence of a lavatory and the cold building in winter months!

A new congregation does not develop in a vacuum. Most of the existing church members understood the need for the development and encouraged it. A few felt uncomfortable with the informal, and at times, noisy style. Early on it was recognized that the monthly slot would not encourage families to experience Easter worship. The decision was made to run an extra service, using the same guidelines, on Good Friday. Attendance at this usually averages around 60, which indicates that Easter, in the broadest sense, is still part of the village year. However, attempts to run a Family Communion on Easter Day were poorly attended. This suggests that these families are concerned that they will find a Eucharist less comfortable. An early attempt to provide a Eucharist as part of 'Service with a Smile ☺' similarly attracted few families. The parish plans to discuss receiving communion before confirmation as a possible way forward for this congregation. It should be noted that baptisms at St Peter's buck the national trend and continue at the same level as they have for the past 25 years.

The development of the new congregation brought greater confidence to the small group that serves as the parochial church council. Having had one success in outreach, the PCC then decided to face the fact that attendance at the traditional harvest service had dwindled. It was proposed to take the format of the very popular carol-singing evening outside the pub and to develop it with a harvest theme. A teacher from the school agreed to organize a group of children to sing some harvest songs, and the lay reader devised a short act of worship that included three harvest hymns, a psalm, a two-minute talk and a prayer. The pub, delighted to welcome the event, advertised a harvest meal at a specially-reduced rate featuring local produce. A new tradition was born and continues with families at its heart. In turn, attendance at the Harvest Festival service has grown as the content has been made more informal, with tea and games for all ages being offered beforehand.

The leaders of St Peter's Church still face a number of challenges – not least in getting others to share leadership. Some of the newly-attending parents chose to join the electoral roll but as yet none will serve on the PCC. They will, however, take responsibility for organizing the refreshments, decorating the church for Christmas and harvest, and contributing to the music group when needed.

The key features of St Peter's that have brought about this story of encouragement are:

- one person with enthusiasm and vision for outreach through well-designed all-age worship;

- consistent support and encouragement from the parish priest;

- another person who has willingly served as churchwarden and PCC secretary as well as offering a general ministry of pastoral care and encouragement;

- committed involvement of the pre-school leader both to 'Service with a Smile ☺' and to building relationships with the young families;

- willingness of the existing congregation to adapt or move aside;

- general acceptance that change was necessary not just to avoid stagnation but to reverse rapid decline;

- good communication and positive relationships.

Questions for discussion

1. In what ways does the description of Brampford Speke differ from a description of your own village or community?

2. Does it matter that this young congregation does not take part in the Eucharist?

3. Is there someone in your village who could take the role of the pre-school leader to provide a friendly link with young families?

Conclusion

Much of this book has been about finding ways of building relationships with children and their families so they can learn about God. Small congregations may find it easier to undertake this task if they look to celebrate and build community, to learn about God and how he is already working in the children with whom they seek to share worship.

Throughout the country, congregations and small groups of Christians are discovering ways to reach out to children. Some have found success at the first attempt, others have had to experiment to find what works in their community. Prayer, research and enthusiasm will lead to a vision for this kind of outreach. Try, or adapt, some of the ideas in this book – don't just put it away on the shelf!

> I will open my mouth in parables, and I will utter hidden things,
> things from of old – what we have heard and known,
> what our fathers have told us.
> We will not hide them from their children;
> we will tell the next generation the praiseworthy deeds of
> the LORD,
> his power, and the wonders he has done.
> He decreed statutes for Jacob and established the law
> in Israel,
> which he commanded our forefathers to teach their children,
> so the next generation would know them, even the children yet
> to be born,
> and they in turn would tell their children.
>
> *Psalm 78* (NIV)

Notes

Introduction

1   Research by Leslie J. Francis and David W. Lankshear, The Impact of Children's Work on Village Church Life' in *Spectrum*, vol. 24, no. 1, Spring 1992.

1 Rural church today

1   DEFRA Rural Strategy: www.defra.gov.uk/rural/strategy/annex_b

2   The Rural Definition was introduced in 2004 as a joint project between the Commission for Rural Communities (CRC – formerly the Countryside Agency), the Department for Environment, Food and Rural Affairs (Defra), the Office for National Statistics (ONS), the Office of the Deputy Prime Minister (ODPM) and the Welsh Assembly.

3   Population Trends in Rural Areas of England 1991–2001, Rural Statistics Unit, Defra, 2002.

4   Social exclusion is a more complex concept than poverty. It considers a wide range of factors such as unemployment or low income, poor living conditions or environment, poor transport and isolation, inequality, poor education, limited access to activities because of poor health or disability, and few social networks.

5   These figures come from the Rural Child Poverty briefing paper, published in 2003 by End Child Poverty, NCH the Children's Charity and the Forum for Rural Children and Young People.

6   Statistics relating to the occurrence of religious loyalty have been produced in the Rural and Urban Area Classification 2004, by the Office for National Statistics, from the 2001 census.

7   Lynda Barley, *Churchgoing Today*, Church House Publishing, 2006.

8   Lynda Barley, *Churchgoing Today*, Church House Publishing, 2006.

4 Belonging and being

1   Leslie J. Francis, Susan H. Jones and David W. Lankshear, 'Baptism Policy and Church Growth in Church of England, Rural, Urban and Suburban Parishes', in *Modern Believing*, vol. 37, no. 3, July 1996.

Resources

General resources for working with children

Organizations and online resources

The best source of specific and local advice for those working in the Church of England is the Diocesan Children's Work Adviser for your area: www.cwanetwork.org.uk/map

Those working in the Methodist tradition can contact www.methodistchildren.org.uk and those working in the Baptist tradition can contact www.baptist.org.uk for advice.

Other organizations with a specific aim of working in rural areas are:

Rural Sunrise, established in 1988, to resource rural churches in mission. It is linked to the Centre for Rural Missions: www.ruralmissions.org.uk/sunrise.htm

The Fellowship for Evangelising Britain's Villages was founded in 1919 and works with all denominations. They have experience of running Village Days and Holiday Bible Clubs. See www.febv.org.uk

Useful books

Eleanor Zuercher, *Not Sunday Not School!*, The Bible Reading Fellowship, 2006 (ISBN 1 84101 490 7), written specifically for those working with rural children.

Margaret Withers, *Where Two or Three*, Church House Publishing, 2004 (ISBN 0 7151 4028 0), written for those working with very small numbers.

Margaret Withers, *Where are the Children?*, The Bible Reading Fellowship, 2005 (ISBN 1 84101 361 7).

Margaret Withers, *Fired Up . . . Not Burnt Out,* The Bible Reading Fellowship, 2001 (ISBN 1 84101 209 2).

Times and seasons

Online resources

For ideas on how not to spend any money during one day, visit www.buynothingday.co.uk

'Posada': details can be found through the Church Army web site: www.churcharmy.org.uk

Information about *Godly Play* and its materials can be found at www.godlyplay.org.uk

The Children's Society provides comprehensive instructions and ideas for leading Christingle celebrations at www.childrenssociety.org.uk

Useful books

Together for a Season: All-Age Resources for Advent, Christmas and Epiphany, Church House Publishing, 2006 (ISBN 0 7151 4062 0) includes material for Christingle and Posada.

Together for a Season: All-Age Resources for Lent, Holy Week and Easter, Church House Publishing, 2007 ISBN 0 7151 4063 5.

John Muir and Betty Pedley, *All-Age Plus Resources*, includes services and activities for spring, harvest, Rogation and other times in the Church's year. They can be contacted at All Age Plus, 8 Whitley Drive, Holmfield, Halifax, HX2 9SJ, or via an Internet search for All Age Plus Resources.

Rites of passage

General and online resources

The Baptism Cube, Church House Publishing, 2006 (ISBN 0 7151 4077 9).

Storykeepers DVD and resources: www.storykeepers.com/marcus.html

The Child Bereavement Trust lists many helpful books for children to read on its web site: www.childbereavement.org.uk

Useful books

Diana Murrie, *My Baptism Book: A Child's Guide to Baptism*, Church House Publishing, 2006 (ISBN 0 7151 4091 4).

The Teddy Horsley books, mentioned in the Bentley Bears story in Chapter 3, are published by Christian Education Publications: www.christianeducation.org.uk

Margery Francis, *Get Ready Go*, Scripture Union, 2005 (ISBN 1 84427 132 3).

It's Your Move, Scripture Union, 2006 (ISBN 1 84427 212 5).

Catherine House, *Where did Grandad Go?*, Barnabas, 2006 (ISBN 1 84101 502 4).

Meg Harper, *Grandma's Party*, Barnabas, 2003 (ISBN 1 84101 341 2) is a story with associated activities to help children going through the bereavement process.

Robert Harrison and Roger Langton, *The Strong Tower*, Scripture Union, 2006 (ISBN 1 84427 122 6) contains stories for tough times, and helpful notes on how to use the book with children.

Belonging and being
Advice and resources on running holiday clubs and missions

Barnabas (part of the Bible Reading Fellowship), Elsfield Hall, 15–17 Elsfield Way, Oxford OX2 8FG: www.barnabasinchurches.org.uk

Scripture Union, 207–209 Queensway, Bletchley, Milton Keynes, MK22 2EB: www.scriptureunion.org.uk

Family Friendly Churches Trust, Wesley Manse, Town Street, Upwell, Wisbech, Cambs PE14 9AD: www.FamilyFriendlyChurches.org.uk

Index